First Light

First Light

Life speaks to us only when we are listening.

Kris Williams

To order additional copies of this book, contact:
Xlibris LLC
1-888-795-4274
www.Xlibris.com
Orders@Xlibris.com
604674

Contents

Where do we go from here?

Reflections by Firelight

First Light

In astronomical terms, *first light* is the first image seen when using a new or upgraded telescope to observe the heavens. While the first images require additional focus and adjustment of the lens to provide the clearest images, they herald the beginning of a new access to information and knowledge never achieved with older technology.

In a conversation about personal transformation, *first light* could also be used to describe a new perspective (or viewpoint) we get of ourselves, others or a life situation resulting from a breakthrough or awakening. An awakening occurs whenever we receive an insight which alters our perception of reality.

Our transformed viewpoint, just like in the world of astronomy, is the new lens by which we relate and react to what happens in the area of life where a breakthrough occurred. And like the telescope, our new perspective can give us an access to workability, ease, and clarity that would otherwise not be available to us.

The new telescopic lens does not dictate what the astronomer sees; it only enhances and improves the clarity of the image provided by the telescope. Consequently, the intention of this book is not to suggest what you should think, feel or believe. It does suggest that we all live inside of self-imposed and in most cases, unconscious limitations in our ability to express (at least to some degree) our nature joy, aliveness and creativity.

What gets in our way is not a smudge on our view of life, but rather the conclusions, conditions and expectations we use to choose what we do about life. It doesn't matter if we allow our joy to be robbed from us by something as ordinary as an upset because traffic was too slow or, the disappointment we feel when looking at our imperfect bodies in a mirror; the outcome is still the same.

As a writer, I like to use everyday life situations to illustrate how we unconsciously set borders and boundaries which, if left unchallenged, affect every aspect of our lives from relationships, to our health and well-being. In some of the short stories we will take a closer look at love, personal choice, our need for perfection, commitments, and our fear of taking chances just to name a few.

Along the way, I will share with you a few personal recollections from my life that gave me an access to a new view, which otherwise would not have be possible. Some of them may even sound like a page taken from your own life, or they may trigger a long-forgotten memory of a person or event that helped create who you are today.

Either way, *First Light* will be a fun journey of self-discovery; so relax, pour yourself a glass of your favorite beverage, and see what is here for you to get.

Kris Williams
July 24, 2013

All of Us

Breaking through our self-imposed limitations begins by challenging our expectations and conclusions about what happens.

Being Human

A group of us were waiting at a bus stop and noticed a man trip over a spot in the concrete where a tree root had pushed up on the sidewalk so much it cracked, leaving a small hump in the concrete.

"Stupid tree," said the man angrily as he righted himself and walked on. Some in our group laughed at the man for getting so angry with a tree that was only doing what trees do.

Then I realized that when I judged the man who yelled at the tree and joined the others in laughter, I was doing what humans do.

It wasn't funny any longer.

What We Don't See

A young man, eager to learn the secret to living a life of peace and abundance, chased after the Sage on the road leading to a town where he will beg for a few coins to buy his next meal. When he finally caught him he asked, "Kind Sage, how can I end the struggle and worry in my life?"

"Walking on this road is just like our walk through life" began the Sage. "You see questions, doubt, desire for excitement and disappointment before you; I see the road leading to the next town. I see it just as it is and as it isn't – nothing more or less."

"When you can be with me on this path, you will see that the peace you seek has always walked with you."

Avoiding Domination

Ever notice how we avoid being dominated?

It's good to avoid being dominated by things that create real harm like addictions, or other behaviors like laziness, aggression, apathy, or prejudice. But when our fear of being harmed is imagined, our avoidance can work against us, create more problems and eventually lead to negative consequences.

It can become a vicious circle.

Most of us avoid things they assume, or fear may be dominating like God, parents, authority, intimacy, commitment, family, etc. In these areas of life our avoidance may kill off any possibility of connection, love, partnership or community.

Avoiding domination is a two-edged sword.

Occasionally, it might be wise to take a look at the things we're avoiding and see if we would really be harmed by allowing them into our life. Giving up our fear is like opening a window. We may find that an open window doesn't always let in crooks or creepy things that go bump in the night.

So, what are you avoiding, and is your avoidance a choice or a habit?

If you can laugh at yourself, it doesn't matter what anyone says about you.

Cracking the Shell

A Sage was sitting with his young student on the bank of a gently flowing stream. "Kind Sage," said the boy, "Do you think humans will ever be able to communicate telepathically?"

Upon which, the Sage reached into his coat pocket and took out a robin's egg he had found that morning by his shack. Placing the egg in the young man's hand he said, "Just as the baby robin believes the whole world exists within the boundaries of its egg shell, so humans see themselves and their life through the filter of their self-imposed limitations."

"While the egg shell protects the robin, so it also limits and constrains. One day, when all is ready, the robin will break through the shell and emerge into a new world where soon he will learn how to fly."

So it is with humans.

Being with Nothing

"I'm so bored," said the young man to the Sage. "There's nothing to do and it's driving me crazy!"

"Yes," smiled the Sage, "that is a problem because we can't DO anything with 'nothing', we can only BE with it."

"When you can BE with nothing and give up resisting—boredom vanishes," said the Sage. "Anytime we can be with what is so in the present, what happens in life no longer becomes a problem."

"That sounds a little weird," laughed the young man. "Of course it does," said the Sage.

The Cloak of Darkness

A young seeker and his Zen master were entering the forest just as nightfall was descending upon them. The strange sounds coming from the darkness caused the young man to walk closer to his master and ask, "I'm afraid of the darkness. Are you also afraid Master?"

"Yes," answered the Master, "Fear is always present." "This haunting is our body's constant fear of death and it will use whatever is available to prevent death from coming. What you feel is the underlying despair and powerlessness which create the strategies we survive with and affects the choices we make in life."

"Beneath every choice, our fear reveals itself and also the secret of our commitments. Have you noticed your commitment to get what you want with the least amount of effort, money or thinking? Or, how you seek out any excitement or diversion to escape the reality of being alone in the present moment?

"Have you ever thought about why you like to avoid feeling guilty, but do the things that make you feel guilty anyway? And, why you avoid taking responsibility for anything that doesn't directly benefit you or what matters to you?"

"Death will come one day that is certain, but life and possibility surround us too," continued the Master. "We transcend fear when we learn to truly be with life as it is in the present and only then will we know the peace of finally seeing who we are and where we belong."

"It is not the darkness itself that is the problem; it is your fear of the unknown that haunts you."

It doesn't matter how good our insurance is, we're not getting out of this alive.

Our Point-of-View

The Sage sat on an old wooden box to rest after walking into town from his small shack a few miles away that he built on the river bank. In the sky above was a rainbow that formed after a rain shower on the other side of a valley ten miles or so west of town.

He heard the people behind him bark orders to the owner of a fruit stand. Resting at the fountain in the center of the town square, one with a statue dedicated to a local hero lost in the last war, was a young mother and her newborn propped up so she could look out from inside her baby carriage.

On the sidewalk one store away was an artist painting a picture of the fountain, people and shops that surrounded the town square. He marveled at the beauty of the rainbow and the innocence of the newborn as the artist made the town square spring to life on his canvas. There was passion in the voices of the customers behind him. Then he noticed that no one but him saw any of it.

The young mother looked at the Sage sitting on an old wooden box in front of her. She noticed how he looked first at the sky, then turned his head as if listening to something, smiled lovingly at her newborn daughter and finally took a few moments watching an artist on the sidewalk. He was in front of the vegetable stand painting something on a stretched canvas that rested on the easel before him. She wondered why the Sage never saw her studying him and why he looked so old and tired. Then she noticed that no one but her saw the old man.

The artist delighted in seeing the sunlight splash upon the water droplets as they were hurled into the afternoon sky by the fountain. He noticed the shadows form slowly on the buildings behind the fountain and how the dark background made the colors of the water droplets sparkle. He hoped to finish his painting before sunset. He thought about including the young mother, her newborn, and the baby carriage in his painting and watched as she stared at the old man across the street who was sitting on a wooden box of some kind. Then he noticed that no one but him saw the sparkling water droplets.

The shop owner tried to be patient with the customers who were complaining about this year's late arrival of sweet corn. He hoped they would leave soon so he could finish putting away a new batch of melons. He noticed an old man sitting on one of his old fruit boxes in front of his stand and wondered if he should give him something to eat.

In another moment the sun will continue to set, the rainbow will begin to fade away, the newborn will fall asleep, and the artist will start packing his paints. The shop owner hands an apple to the Sage sitting on an old wooden box. One moment in time passes into another and with it, our point of view.

While each moment contains everything available to us in the universe; our view will forever be limited by the filter of our personal life experience. Therefore, our viewpoint is, by its essential nature, incomplete, subjective and limited. Such is the inherent fallacy of viewpoints.

And the reason why we should never trust the information we use to judge and label others is the whole truth about them.

The Path of Least Resistance

There are two ways of dealing with things in our life that aren't working.

We can either sweep them under the carpet until next time (and there's always a next time) or, take responsibility and clean up the mess.

If we know that taking the easy way out, while appealing at the time, usually leads to waste and regret . . .

Why do we continue to do it?

What's The Problem?

Animals don't have a problem with life because for them, life is just the way it is right now. Surviving is not something they've learned to escape from or find a solution for. There are no victims in the animal kingdom because they never express pity for either themselves or others.

Animals don't remember the pain of last year, they just react to what nature provides in the present moment. For them the future doesn't exist so there's no need to make plans or change anything.

Humans are unique. We have evolved brains that remember the unrelenting harshness and pain of living. Survival for us involves avoiding the harsh realities of life. For humans the cruelty, discomfort, burdens, isolation, confusion, boredom, fear, uncertainty, emptiness, chaos and, agony are problems that can and must be solved.

The human brain always lets us know then we have solved one of these problems because we are rewarded with feelings of pleasure. Comfort, excitement, safety, and certainty feel *'good'* and allow us to experience pleasure. Pleasure is our solution for the realities of life. Pleasures which can be easily accessed by most of the wonderful inventions we have at our fingertips. Accessible that is, if we have the money to obtain them.

Our unique ability to avoid life as it is leaves us addicted to both comfort and the pursuit of pleasure. This pursuit gives our life purpose and meaning. And yet, this never seems to solve the problem. The harshness and pain of life continue to haunt and rests just below the surface of our awareness. Ironically, the harshness of life is the only thing we can ever really be sure of.

The solution is there is no solution. What we think is a problem requires no solution because it is life as it is right now. Yes, we can continue to escape them momentarily or, choose another option. We can learn to be with the harsh realities of life rather than avoid, resist or anesthetize ourselves when confronted by them.

Every now and then make time to go visit a forest. Leave behind your car, cell phone, cigarettes, music and Tylenol. Enter the forest without expectations or fear. As you walk, notice the different sounds and smells. Feel your connection to nature. Let go of the noise in your head and just listen to the stillness. When you are totally surrounded by the forest, stop and look around.

This is what reality looks like without solutions.

All We Have

All we have is what we can see, hear, touch, smell and taste in this moment and our perception of them.

We can have a debate over perception for a thousand years and still not see what is right in front of us as it truly is.

Our consciousness is like a space that contains our life. Our spaciousness is only separated from all there is by the lens we use at this moment. Perhaps, there is only one consciousness as there is only one space that contains all there is.

Questioning our perception transforms the lens by which we view what happens in life and to what extent we are related to it.

If you want a peaceful life, notice your expectations. The path of peace is littered with expectations never acted upon because they are treated as a consideration rather than the truth.

Imagination

Every child uses it to create worlds where they can be anyone and go anywhere they want.

Later, we use it to understand, react to, and create a conceptual image of the world we live in. Imagination is a mental platform we use to help us deal with the people, events and life situations occurring outside the space of what we can physically see, hear, touch, smell and taste.

Over time, we gradually begin to believe this virtual world, with its own unique knowledge, images, rules, boundaries, meanings and relationships, is the truth. Unless someone or something awakens us, we can spend our entire life living in the world of our imagination.

If you don't think this is so, notice that you are using imagination to understand and draw conclusions about what I am telling you now.

Imagination is so interwoven into our daily lives; it is hard to distinguish when we are there and when we are not. If you are not aware of what is happening in and around the physical space of your body, you are probably somewhere in your imagination dreaming about work, tonight's dinner, fears you have or things that need to be done.

Children know when they are using imagination, and they know their imagined world is simply that; an imagined world. When Mom calls them to dinner, they close the door to their imagination and walk away.

Adults shouldn't take their imagined world so seriously. While it can help us shape our future and fulfill passion, it can also conjure up rationalization for starting wars, arguments and actions that distract us from noticing the beauty right in front of our eyes.

Until we learn the facts by actually experiencing the space beyond our senses, it's all just our imagination telling us what might be out there and what it all means.

If you want to see an optimist cry, sit him down in front of a slot machine and watch him play with $20 of his own money.

Beings Becoming (read this one carefully)

It is natural for Beings like us to want to Be something. The question is; what shall we Be?

When our past experiences cease to remain in the past and we allow them to live in the present as our conclusions, judgments and expectations, we become our past. We become our story about that little girl or boy who learned to avoid being laughed at, bullied or rejected.

When our future ceases to be our passion because we allow fear to motivate our actions, we become that shy little boy who never kissed his sweetheart or that sad little girl who never asked for what she wanted.

When our past and future remain concepts, considerations and intentions kept in the background of our continuous mental chatter, we get to choose new ways of being. It is our Beingness that breathes life into them and makes them real – who we are.

So, what does the present look like right now, your life story, or your passion?

Responding & Waiting

I spend most of my time responding.

Responding to people who request something from me, responding to people waiting on me to make a decision or take some action to move things along.

It's like working on an assembly line where I'm constantly sorting the mail as it comes to me. If I spend too much time on one piece the rest starts backing up so I sometimes make a quick decision just to keep things moving.

The problem with my way of dealing with the backlog is I miss really great opportunities.

Eventually, my shift is over and I've moved a lot of mail, but also overlooked some possibilities.

Perhaps I need to learn how to spot opportunities when they pass by instead of just moving things along until my shift ends.

The main reason we miss opportunities is we forget to look for them.

I also spend most of my time waiting.

Waiting to speak, waiting on someone to respond, waiting on my food to cook, waiting for information, waiting for the driver ahead of me to get going, waiting for life to give me what I want, when I want it.

What I've discovered about waiting is it's just another form of resisting what is happening or, in my case, not happening in the present moment.

It's like planting seeds in a garden. I plant one seed, then when nothing happens immediately, I plant another, and another and then another. By this time, I'm so frustrated, confused and weary I just give up.

I still need to learn patience, trust and the true nature of seeds. My garden is growing; I just need to keep in mind that it may not always grow at a speed that suits my ego—and, it's ok.

Perfect!

Finally I park the car, grab my small cooler, towel, and chair then it's a short walk to find a place to watch the sunrise on Ft. Myers Beach. After taking that first sip of my tall caramel macchiato I think to myself; *this is perfect*. Some other guy is lining up a putt on the 5th green at Pebble Beach Golf Club 2,000 miles away and is thinking the exact same thing at that exact moment.

How can perfection be in two places at the same time?

If you stop to think about it, our notion of perfection controls a lot of what we do, spend money on, and strive for in life. And, if we let it, our desire to finally arrive at, achieve, get to, master or acquire that perfect place, time, possession, relationship or status will drive us crazy. By crazy I mean being unable to experience our natural joy and connectedness.

Perhaps there is no one perfect place to be, one perfect time to live, one perfect career, real estate, political party, people to know, view of the ocean, etc. And if there isn't, what does this say about our desire to achieve perfection? Who decides what perfection is anyway?

If our collective ideals of perfection are just what everyone buys into so we can belong or be accepted and it really doesn't exist, why do we continue to allow this to define who we are? Belonging or being accepted is a priority and for sure, it's our way of fitting in. It's also our way of deciding who we accept, and who we choose to be our friend.

We often expect our friends to think like we think, act like we act, and always want to do what we want to do when we want to do it. When we hear a difference of opinion, decision or choice as a rejection I think we violate what true friendship is and can be.

A true friend may not agree with what you say, but will always appreciate who is speaking. And when you don't agree on where to eat lunch, you don't go just to appease your friend and then feel depressed because you didn't get your way; you go because it doesn't matter who decided or where you go, what really matters is that you're together. When it's not all about "me", true friendship has a way of turning the whole world into a playground.

Our happiness and fulfillment, when based on ideals of perfection, are only conditional and limited until our realization that we are the problem: we are getting in our own way. The chains that stop us, the mud that slows us down, and the veil that limits our sight are fashioned by the same hands that will eventually free us.

What we find out about ourselves when we let go of our conditions and expectations is someone who is naturally connected to life and belongs everywhere. Until this transcendence occurs for us, we will continue to reject those we love and never truly enjoy the warmth of being totally accepted by or accepting of anyone.

So, that's just the way it is right now and it's perfect, or not, depending on your point of view.

*If you want to change some aspect of your life,
you cannot begin from there or someday.
Begin from where you are.*

Obligations

When the things that need to be handled become nothing more than obstacles keeping us from reaching a made-up finish line where we are no longer responsible, it's time to examine why they are important to us.

It's ok to drop something when it no longer works for you, and renew a commitment for doing what does.

A commitment without joy is an empty promise that soon becomes a burden carried on the back of regret and resignation.

What good can come from this?

Integrity

Integrity is an important ingredient for honoring our commitments in life.

If you've heard about Landmark Education or even better, attended one of their seminars, somewhere during the evening or weekend you'll hear the phrase: "Without integrity, nothing works." And it's true; you can't sit on a chair with only two legs or become a lawyer without first passing the bar exam.

Failure to keep promises, to ourselves or others, leaves loose ends in our life that rob us of our power until they are cleaned up and resolved.

We often make commitments we have no intention of fulfilling on. We do this out of a feeling of obligation, conflict avoidance, or any number of reasons that make sense at the time. Some of the commitments which motivate us are undeclared and hidden just below the surface of our consciousness. They are left-overs from a long forgotten decision about what we want or need.

When we find that we are upset with ourselves or others, defensive, or make excuses when confronted with our pretense, it is probably because we are out of integrity or being prevented from fulfilling on a commitment.

The interesting thing about integrity and commitment is that we are *always* honoring a commitment, even one we may not remember.

So, if you are out of integrity with a commitment you know about, look deeper and see what you might *REALLY* be committed to.

You may not like what you see, but the new view will transform your life.

The Good and Bad of It

When we bring judging, conclusions and expectations into the realm of relationships, our natural inclination is to place people, places and things into good and bad categories.

Often, the evidence seems so real we are mystified when someone else has a differing opinion. Relationships are often based solely on how our definitions of *good* and *bad* agree or disagree with the other person.

Over the course of our lifetime, the reason a conclusion was formed has long been forgotten. No one can remember why we decided it was good or bad to react in the way we do in a given situation. Fortunately, our definitions of *good* and *bad*, has the possibility to transform when someone challenges the context or evidence.

Challenging our notion of what is good or bad takes vigilance and courage. Vigilance helps us watch for the lustful thrill when things go our way or the upset, pain and agony when they don't. Courage helps us start something new, to go beyond the safe haven of past judgments.

When we dislodge a label, we open a space to relate to the person, place or thing with a new clarity. When we are no longer forced to automatically react from a mental construct we are free to allow the future to determine the outcome rather than the past. Life in this context becomes an adventure of discovery, wonder and gratitude.

In the world of personal transformation, this is called a breakthrough or an awakening.

When you have a little time, write down a few of the people, places or things in your life that you have given a good or bad label. Next, think about why they are good or bad. Finally, look to see what evidence has been used to justify your conclusion.

Until things change, this is the way it is . . .
. . . and when things change, this will still be the way it is.

My Transformed Friends Out Here

One of the attributes I like best about transformed people is they never act like they've got it all figured out.

They are always open to seeing another view and challenging their expectations and conclusions.

I'm amazed at their ability to constantly reinvent themselves

That Person Sitting Next to You

Who Are They Really?

When we enter into a new relationship, the other person is not only who we want them to be for us, but also who they are for themselves. Who they are for themselves is rarely revealed to us because of who we want them to be.

Knowing this, what must be done to *really* know the other person?

Keeping Score

Ever notice how we like to keep score?

We keep a mental tally of who owes us for stuff we do, say and give. Most of us do these things out of unconditional kindness, but somewhere in the background the numbers are still automatically adding up.

What's funny is we always know who owes us, but unless we feel obligated because the tally is greatly in someone else's favor, we don't see who we owe.

It's just comes with being human I suppose.

At some time in even our most intimate relationships this same issue often arises. We keep score to ensure we are making a safe investment of our love, time and energy.

One of the problems with keeping score in a close relationship is that we carry around an expectation the score must always be tied in order for the relationship to be working. It rarely works out this way so upset, suspicion and resignation result.

When we can put aside the score and collaborate on a common purpose, it's possible to form a lasting partnership. Knowing this, is it time for an honest conversation about what's really important rather than who made the bed this morning?

The Other Guy

Ever notice how we expect everyone to be perfect except us?

They must always be on time, have the repair done when we get there, say just the right thing or, never interrupt when we are speaking. Our list of complaints about *everyone else* goes on and on.

Sometimes we forget they are human too.

The guy you honk at who is staring into space when the traffic light turns green was *you* earlier this morning.

And who was the lady who made a mistake when counting out change at the restaurant?

Yep, you guessed it.

It was you.

I love you!
They need to hear it and you need to say it.

Who's Responsible for Happiness?

A young lady was riding on a bus sitting next to an older woman. As she gazed out at the passing scenery she began to cry. "What's troubling you?" asked the older women. "I'm sad because I broke up with my boyfriend," said the young lady while drying her eyes. "I can't seem to find a relationship that works. Either he's unhappy and leaves or I get upset and walk away."

"Most people think that a lasting relationship requires a lot of work, but it's easy if you can accomplish a few simple tasks," said the older woman. "What's that?" asked the young lady.

"Well, first you must put aside all of the hopes and fears you brought into the relationship. This is so you can see the other person as they really are, and not as you want them to be."

"Next," said the older woman with a smile, "You must have a conversation about what you want from the relationship, what you are committed to giving and what you expect from him. Finally, you must understand that he is not responsible for your happiness—you are."

"But I thought we get married so we can find happiness," barked the young lady, who rolled her eyes and cast a halfhearted smile in the woman's direction.

"When he is no longer responsible for carrying the burden of your happiness, he will be free to be your friend and partner. So it seems to me you have a choice to make young lady," said the older woman with a chuckle, "Whether you want to marry a donkey or, your friend."

A Simple Choice

Regarding our relationships: Have you ever noticed those moments when he says just the right thing that lets you know he still loves you, or you count on her to cook a delicious meal when your parents came to visit and everything turned out perfectly?

These are precious moments not only because they reveal our love for each other but also, because after we've gotten what we want, when, and how we wanted it, there is a moment of calm—a brief stillness is present.

When we notice and listen to this stillness there is an opening, or space where we get to choose what happens next.

We can begin the *what about me* cycle all over again, or take the time to be grateful, to really know the people in our lives, to look deeper at those who usually only get a passing glance.

We can choose to consider what they need and where our contribution could make a difference.

Thinking and Knowing

A young man sat by the side of a road very confused. An old Sage was passing by at that moment, saw the distressed young man, and asked what was troubling him.

"My betrothed says she loves me, but how will I ever really know for sure?"

The old man smiled and said, "You will never know the secrets of her heart while doubt stands in the way. Put your thoughts and fears aside and in the stillness that remains, simply hold her hand and look into her eyes."

"For it is through stillness that you will share the secrets of her heart, not thought."

True friendship has a way of turning the whole world into a playground.

Love by Any Other Name

What is the true nature and purpose of love?

We humans often use the word love to describe our relationship with the people, places or things. Ever hear someone say, "I love going to Ft. Myers", "I just love her dress" or, "I loved that movie"? We have all heard love used when describing our highest level of affection, degree of closeness or familiarity. It seems an important ingredient of the things we love is their ability to provide us with an experience of pleasure, satisfaction, and emotional security.

At the other end of the love spectrum, we use negative terms like hate to describe our indifference to anything which we feel is repulsive or fails to give us what we want, when we want it. Phrases like: "I hate the way he treats her" or, "I hate that smell" are familiar to all of us.

Have you ever seen a relationship where one person is an alcoholic and the other is the enabler? Or, where one person physically abuses the other yet the victim continues to stay in the marriage? This is because love is sometimes confused with feelings of dependency. However great our need to be loved or fear of being alone, when we confuse love with an addictive relationship, it is a delusion which can easily lead to dangerous consequences.

In fact, the word love is tossed around so freely in our culture its true meaning and purpose has been diluted to the point where we really don't know what love is or how to recognize it when we see it. So, if love is not a term of endearment or reason for enabling a dependent relationship, what is it?

My research into the true nature of love took me on a journey through dictionaries and writings of scholars in philosophy, religion and spirituality. I learned that the scholars believe we experience two types of love; natural love and divine love.

They define natural (subjective) love as the feelings of affection and familiarity we all experience throughout our lifetimes. These are the same feelings that are aroused in us when someone we are attracted to calls on the telephone, texts or visits. When we say that natural love is subjective, this means our love is dependent to how we benefit emotionally from that relationship. In other words, we love how the person, place or thing makes us feel emotionally.

If the love we feel is subjective it is primarily concerned with protecting or validating our own internal, emotional priorities. When this happens, these same priorities tend to objectify the people, places and things we are attracted to. Have you ever seen someone take a bite of an apple and say, "I love the taste of apples"? They are connecting emotionally with the taste of the apple rather than the apple itself.

Simply stated, natural love is generally the outcome of our personal dependency on pleasure, satisfaction, excitement and security rather than the source of them.

If we are in a relationship based solely on mutual validation and pleasure which can easily lead to dependency—is this really love?

Not according to the scholars.

They say divine love is the source of empathy, compassion and true friendship. Divine love is a healing force that leaves us aware of our connection with all life. The primary difference between natural (subjective) love and divine love exists in the nature of the relationship between the lovers. Where natural love is about 'me', divine love is about 'us'. Going back to the example of the apple, divine love would be the connection we have with the apple itself rather than the pleasure we experience from it.

When two people share divine love, they dance together in a level of intimacy that is always fresh and new; beyond time and space. True love is risky business. We cannot play it safe and find it; we must be willing to risk it all.

We must be willing to give up our judgments, personal desires and expectations and begin to focus our attention on the source of the attraction in the present moment. Only in the present can we truly be related, experience compassion for and fully know someone or something outside ourselves.

In the stillness of the present moment we instantly sense a new intimacy where two become one. In this new space of oneness, love lifts us up and opens a new world of possibility. If we listen closely, it will tell us what to say or do to remove limitations, expand horizons and heal the past. Sometimes only a simple smile or a gentle hug is necessary—that is all.

This then is the true nature and purpose of love; that when we consciously prepare a space of presence and stillness, it uses us to create abundance and more love.

Love by any other name is not Love.

When Problems Arise

The people in our life are not some static image made up of all our information about them. They come to us with their own dynamic momentum consisting of views, fears, expectations and life experiences.

Some of the experiences are unresolved or incomplete and may cause problems that can secretly sabotage the health of our relationship with them.

Knowing this, how can we support their completion?

Only Love knows . . .

How Relationships Impact Us

We are surrounded by relationships, by people who say they love us.

Some use their love to make us weak; some use their love to make us strong.

So the question we could ask to define a relationship is, "Do I feel weak or strong?"

And the question we must ask to have a breakthrough in a relationship is, "Does my love leave you weak or strong?"

Both questions can create an access to intimacy if answered authentically.

What we find out about ourselves when we let go of our conditions and expectations is someone who is naturally connected with others and belongs everywhere.

Confronting Reality

Have you ever been in a life situation with a friend, colleague or family member when you suddenly realize your prediction of what motivates them to act in a certain way is totally wrong?

It's very humbling, especially when you find that you've been relating to them from this context for years in some cases.

Makes me wonder who I have been doing this with and what the impact has been on them and our relationship.

Reality has a great way of reminding us of how little we actually know about the other person.

Someone Special

Think of someone special in your life; a wife, husband, significant other, a best friend, or even your weird cousin will do.

Can you remember the exact moment when you knew without a doubt that you loved them?

Yes, that's the moment I'm talking about, but don't stop there—it's time for action.

Go tell them right now! Yep, don't wait another second . . .

They need to hear it and you need to say it.

Their First Breath

Our children work so hard to prove themselves, to be worthy of our blessing and respect.

What they don't know is we are already proud of them, already respect and bless them.

They won us over with their first breath and with their first smile we were captured for life.

If we only take on something new because it is safe, logical and rational we will never take on anything new.

How You Know

"I know you love me," said a husband to his wife one sunny afternoon on Ft. Myers Beach.

"How?" asked his wife.

"Because," he said with a smile, "Every time I look into your eyes, they tell me."

Simply Delightful!

Our moments together should not be a burden or something too familiar, tolerated only to satisfy a past obligation, habit, or polite acknowledgement.

When we meet, our togetherness should be delightfully joyous, as if no one else exists in the universe but us; it should be an experience of discovery as we celebrate each other and breathe in that moment as if it was our last.

A great relationship is simple and simply delightful!

The Joy of the Other

There is a natural joy we experience by being with another person in the present as if you are meeting them for the first time (even when you actually are) and receiving them without judgment or expectation.

Our choice to hang on every word they say as if they might reveal a clue to uncovering a hidden treasure rewards us with a jewel that can never be lost or taken from us.

That jewel is friendship.

Just as the baby robin believes the whole world exists within the boundaries of its egg shell, humans view their life through the filter of their self-imposed limitations.

Being a Parent

Parents often have great advice to give their children. This is possible not because they have followed their own advice, but because they didn't and lived to tell about it.

Are They Still the One?

One sure way to tell if your marriage or a significant relationship is in good shape is to imagine being single right now and seeing your spouse for the first time in a night club, store or church.

Would you still pick him or her? Or, would you move on?

If the answer is Yes; acknowledge why it's working.

If it's No; look and see what's missing and discuss what could make a difference.

If it's Hell No!—Declare what you want and create a plan to get there.

When it comes to keeping the relationship fresh and new, whose responsibility is it and what judgment, grudge or expectation are you willing to give up to achieve it?

Where do we go from here?

Where Are You Going?

Someone once said; "Without a precise destination all paths lead to confusion."

We will have less difficulty making a life-changing decision or choosing the right path when we can say precisely what we want at the end of that journey.

What do you want for your life, and do you have the courage to declare it for yourself?

Reinventing Ourselves

A young man, resigned to the notion that his life would remain uninspiring and joyless, sought out the Sage for advice and counsel.

After explaining his predicament in great detail, he looked into the patient eyes of the Sage and asked "How can I bring more excitement and passion into my life?"

"The notion that your life is uninspiring is one you created long ago. Who you are today is the unintended culmination of all your conclusions and decisions about how life is for you. Because it was you who created them, it is you who must reinvent who you want to be," began the Sage.

"If you want more excitement, be exciting. If you want more joy, be joyous. We have little control over what happens in life, but about who we are being-if you can imagine it, anything is possible."

*A commitment without joy is an empty
promise that soon becomes a burden carried
on the back of regret and resignation.*

Questions & Answers

While eating lunch in a local restaurant, a woman was complaining to her mother that she was frustrated over never being able to stick to her diet and exercise plan for very long.

Then she overheard a reporter on the TV in the restaurant interviewing a Buddhist Monk who said . . .

"It's natural for humans to only take action or change their behavior when something has gone wrong or needs immediate attention. Choosing to take action when nothing is wrong, because it's the right thing to do leads to self-mastery and extraordinary results." Nodding her head in approval, she smiled and took another bite of her salad.

Life speaks to us only when we are listening.

Trying Something New?

Opportunities for trying something new are all around us. Taking a chance by saying hello to someone who doesn't fit on your list as '*our*' type of person, or taking a moment to be kind even when no one is looking, are ways that life opens doors for us.

We are responsible for noticing the opportunity and having the courage to walk through the open door. Thinking we already understand how life is and how it works is one sure way of shutting down what's available.

If we only take on something new because it is safe, logical and rational we will never take on anything new. Innovation, extraordinary results, and breakthroughs are found by following a different path.

High-stakes Gambling

I was in Las Vegas recently and spent a lot of time just observing gamblers in the Paris Hotel & Casino. One night I watched as a young man lost all of his money at one of the blackjack tables. Dejected, he went to the nearest ATM and got another $200 and headed back to the blackjack table. I overheard him sigh and mutter to himself, "I don't know what to do—I give up."

Then, when it seemed he had lost all hope, given up his desire to win, and was forced to allow fate to run its course, he calmly looked at the dealer and said, "I need a 21." (This, in blackjack terms is a perfect winning hand.)

He asked without a hint of doubt or fear, ready to accept whatever happened next.

The first card the dealer dealt him was a King, and the next an Ace, which together equal 21. I know what you're thinking, getting a winning hand had nothing to do with his attitude; he could've just as easily lost as he had done previously.

Fortunately, we don't live in a casino where the odds are always stacked against us.

In our daily lives we constantly take chances on how we invest our time, money and love on everything from what we'll do on Saturday night to who we marry. Unlike our experience in the casino, we can actually improve our odds by consciously making informed choices without the distraction of fear or anxiety.

An informed choice, without the distraction of fear, creates the possibility of success and leaves us with the confidence to face an uncertain future with power and freedom.

So, how do you like *your* odds?

*An imagined fear is like running out
of a burning theater that is not on fire.
Why not stick around and watch what happens?*

Safe and Sound

Having just bought a new 28 foot fishing boat, Patrick decided to test it out on the 178 nautical miles between Miami, Florida and Nassau, Bahamas. He carefully and methodically packed everything needed to live on his boat for two weeks while he enjoyed fishing for Blue Marlin in the deep waters off shore. Everything seemed in order.

The problem was he never made it to Nassau. About 90 miles from Miami his motor suddenly quit, and with it the radio he could've used to call for help. He exhausted the boat's batteries trying to restart the engine and didn't think to bring a spare. So, for the rest of that day, and the next three days, he just drifted in the Atlantic Ocean hoping he would be spotted by a passing plane or other fishing boats.

By the end of the third day panic began to have its way with him, and that night he prayed for the first time in years.

Then as the sun was beginning to set on the evening of the fourth day, a miracle happened. Off in the distance he saw what looked like an island. He frantically reached for a small paddle and began to help steer his boat so it would drift close by the island and possibly beach the boat. Hours passed while he paddled furiously, his boat slowly drifting closer and closer to the island. Finally, around midnight, his boat touched down on a white sandy beach lined by palm trees and hibiscus plants in full bloom.

Immediately, he began removing his supplies from the boat to a small clearing chosen among the palm trees. With his supplies organized and neatly stacked, he next started collecting the branches, leafs and other items found on the ground to build a small lean-to. When he had everything safely under the lean-to, and with just enough room left so he had a dry place to sleep, he sat down beneath a palm tree and looked at the moonlight as it danced on the ocean.

More tired than anytime he cared to remember, he drifted off to sleep wondering how long he would wait to be rescued and if his supplies would last. That night a light rain fell upon his lean-to, but he slept so soundly he never noticed.

The sound of a coconut falling to the ground beside his lean-to forced him awake just as sun light was creeping over the horizon. Staring out on the area surrounding his camp, he thought for a moment and then decided that today he would build a fence around his campsite to keep out any intruders.

Feverously he cut and dug holes for each post, used the last of his string to lash together the palm leafs and finally finished completing the last three foot section of his fence. Latching the gate behind him, he stepped back and marveled at his work. Now, waiting to be rescued was the only task left to do.

Sometime around noon on the seventh day he heard a helicopter engine whining overhead, anxiously he watched as the Coast Guard pilot landed on the beach in front of him. "This is private property!" shouted the pilot, "Who gave you permission to park your boat here and camp?"

"Camp" shouted Patrick, "My boat landed here after drifting for over three days in the ocean. I've been waiting for seven days for someone to rescue me!"

"Get in," said the pilot with a smile, "I want to show you something."

The whirling helicopter blades carried them first ten, then fifty, then a hundred feet into the sky above the beach. As they ascended, slowly the entire shoreline of Miami Beach became visible including a mansion on the other side of the small island where his boat had landed. For the last seven days he had been marooned on a private island just 5 miles off the shore of Miami Beach.

"Why didn't you at least try to walk around the island to see what was there?" asked the pilot. "I really don't know," he responded, "I had supplies and I was protected by my fence so I never even thought about it."

That's just like us humans, thought the pilot, *so much available to us and yet, so little that our self-imposed boundaries allow us to explore.*

Workability

A plan, strategy or action is thought to possess *workability* when it achieves the intended result.

When some area of our life is not working, we tend to look for flaws in our plan of action or some cause *over there.*

We should also look at our intention to see if it is achievable or realistic.

We want to feel confident, secure, satisfied, and fulfilled by pursuing that perfect body, home, job or bank account and yet; when we have finally them, our life still never seems to work for very long.

Why is this?

Getting There

Driving a car to an appointment is a lot like trying to accomplish a goal in life. We start out knowing where we want to go and how we want to get there. Then something happens to delay, constrain or distract us. Immediately, most of us start blaming ourselves, someone else or Murphy's Law for the doom that must surely befall us.

It seems like once again we are confronted with the possibility of not accomplishing what we set out for, being responsible for disappointing someone or worse; being known as a person who can't be counted on. So, what's the best way to get through all of this turmoil?

Being a pessimist has some value, but won't work because even though they consider all of the ways their plan might fail, they never really expect their plan to succeed, so they don't venture out in the first place.

Being an optimist has some value, but works only to the extent that nothing happens to block their progress. Their confusion causes so much delay when something adverse does happen, they may also never reach their goal.

A pragmatist checks to see if he has enough gas, maps, water to drink, etc. and then allows enough extra time to handle unexpected roadblocks that might happen. His courage gives him the confidence a pessimist lacks, his logic quiets confusion while quickly creating an alternative plan that the optimist lacks.

Which one would describe how you reach, or fail to reach your goals?

We have so much available to us and yet, so little that we allow ourselves to explore.

Human Conflict

We argue, debate, and protect our viewpoint as if there can be only one winner.

The result is we all lose.

What heights could our conversations reach without winners and losers?

The Present Moment

To some degree, all of us are alert and aware of our emotions, reactions, actions and decisions about what happens in the present moment. We usually are not aware that the present is distinct or separate from our automatic past-based mental reactions.

When we begin to notice that the present is the space in which our reactions occur, new possibilities and choices become available. One nice outcome from living in the present is that even ordinary tasks, like washing the dishes can be done with joy and aliveness simply by thinking about them differently.

The present is also a space to create in. Some of us create a better, faster way to travel inside the same vicious circle. Some create a new destination like workability, contribution or abundance.

Which are you creating?

Defiance

I've always had a problem with doing a chore or donating time when it is heard like an order or feels like someone is trying to dominate me.

On the other hand, I like doing chores or donating time or money when it is my idea. I've learned the hard way that resisting doesn't work and leads to frustration and poor results.

One solution is to give up resisting and listen to the request as a good idea I should've had on my own but missed. In other words, make their suggestion my idea. This takes putting me on the other side of the conversation and seeing the request from their perspective.

I've discovered this strategy opens the door to partnership rather than conflict and upset.

Once you learn that our conclusions about life are all made up, it's easy to reinvent yourself.

Rollercoasters

Rollercoasters are fun.

The anticipation we feel waiting in line, the suspense that grows when over—hearing stories from others in line about how scared they were the first time they rode it; and the screams coming from somewhere *up there* make it all seem real.

Your heart starts pounding when the safety bar snaps into position and you hear the "click-click-clicking" sound as the coaster inches its way to the top. "Is it ever going to get up there?" everyone says out loud.

Then, after a moment of hesitation at the top, you get the first glimpse of the terror waiting below.

Someone challenges you to keep your hands in the air. Not wanting to appear scared, ever so slowly you feel your hands letting go of the safety bar and timidly reaching skyward. Now the screams heard down below are coming from the seat right next to you!

Suspended on the brink of death, now you know the thrill of being alive, not knowing what will happen next and it's always the same, always like the first time. Somehow, we manage to survive and brag to our friends that it wasn't as bad as everyone let on.

Wouldn't it be awesome to feel this way when we first get out of bed every morning?

What a ride that would be . . .

Reflections by Firelight

Wisdom

To the intellectual, words coming from the wise sound silly, foolish and naïve. This is because wisdom can never be communicated in words. Wisdom uses words to point to that which speaks to us from beyond thought.

The truth is . . . all we have is each other.

Life Goes Humming Along

The more each day unfolds with equal regularity, the more I seem to miss opportunities to experience the big things like the sunrise, spring flowers starting to bloom in my yard, and the color of Karen's eyes.

I wonder what else I might be missing.

Time

What happened, what is happening, and what might happen that our identity (ego) has a story about which means nothing and reveals everything about us.

Fear

When our mind perceives that we are in danger, our brain reacts by pumping adrenaline into all areas of our body to increase heart rate, blood flow and alertness in support of our flight or fight response.

Our perception may be real, like almost being struck by another car or imagined, like not knowing what's going to happen when asked to meet with your boss. Most of our imagined fears result from experiences in our past which we don't want to repeat. An example of this could be being fired from a job, being laughed at, being rejected by someone you care about or, personal failure.

The interesting thing about allowing fear to dictate how we respond is that whether we act aggressively or passively (fight or flight) both reactions get in the way of extraordinary results or performance. Our fight response leaves us tense, stressed and rigid which can kill off possibility. Being submissive forces us to retreat mentally or shy away from danger which limits our view of opportunities.

Fear is either past or future-based. It may help you react quickly and decisively in a physically dangerous encounter, but in other areas of life that require rhythm, balance and collaboration in the *present moment*, fear just gets in our way.

We can't move past fear by trying to replace it by conjuring up some other emotion or chanting positive mantras. Extraordinary performance requires us to be fully grounded in the present moment.

What shows up when we move past fear (by being present) is our nature joy, courage and aliveness. All of which are ingredients for the possibility of success.

One strategy for dealing with a fear is to breathe deeply three or four times, focus attention on feeling your body and then ask yourself mentally, "Is there a real danger here?"

If the answer that returns is" No", allow yourself to have fun at what you are doing. Why run out of a burning theater that is not on fire? It's ok to stick around and enjoy the show.

Waiting is just another form of resisting what is happening or not happening in the present moment.

A Leaf Has Two Sides

It seems like life is vicious and intolerable; then a friend calls on the phone, a child smiles at you, or a check arrives in the mail—things start looking up.

Life has a way of kicking us in the butt and handing us a pillow to sit on all at the same time.

What an adventure!

Cultivating a Still Mind

Most of us think that meditation is sitting in a certain position, regulating breath and repeating mantras. All of which are supposed to bring about a state of enlightenment. This is partly true and also partly false.

Anytime and anywhere we take a few moments to relax, breathe deeply, focus our attention on our bodies and be with whatever is there in the present moment without judging we are meditating.

You might be amazed at the positive benefits of cultivating a still mind and having a friendly relationship with the present.

The Best Grandpa Ever!

I was a 12 year old boy fishing with his Grandpa on Lake Wawasee on a Tuesday afternoon. I was hoping to catch "the big one" when a 10 pound northern pike took my lure.

Getting him to the boat was the most exciting time of my life. It seemed like I fought for an hour, but at last my Grandpa grabbed the landing net, placed it in the water, and I guided my trophy gently into its grasp.

Then, with a sudden twist of its head and flip of its tail it tore a hole in the net and disappeared into murky depths below. In an instant I was the victim of a 30-year old landing net that had long since served its purpose.

He saw the sadness on my face and knew what we had to do. We sped back to shore, ran up the bank to the garage and repaired the netting. Then, for the next hour we fished up and down that same area of the lake in an attempt to reclaim my prize.

Realizing at last that our effort was useless, the words "Guess he got away Grandpa" filled the air between us. He nodded his head in approval and we headed home.

Neither of us ever spoke about it again.

But at age 62, I finally see that my 64 year-old Grandpa would've stayed out on that lake all night if necessary to erase the sadness he saw on that little boy's face.

Yep, he loved me that much.

Sadly, I never thanked him for all the tenderness and compassion he showed me that day. But whenever possible, I try to show the world the valuable lesson I learned from him that afternoon on Lake Wawasee. I was blessed to have such an awesome Grandpa.

I pray my life will be worthy of his compassion.

*I love those wonderfully blissful moments in life when
I don't have anything to complain about.*

Problem is . . . they only happen when I'm asleep.

Did He Know Then?

Surrender comes in a gentle phrase, "Father, into thy hands I commend my spirit."

All watch as His blood steadily drips to the ground; each drop is like a teardrop shed without regret for all of us on that cloudy afternoon outside Jerusalem.

Did He know then about the countless millions that would remember this day and find strength from His sacrifice? Did He know then about those who would be healed in His name and find salvation from His words? Did He know then about the wars fought to honor Him, or the millions who would die calling to Him with their last breath?

We will never know.

Perhaps His time on the cross was just like any other dying man gasping for life. Maybe He didn't know then about the world that would spring forth from His simple words, spoken to the poor, and all who followed Him into the hills overlooking the Sea of Galilee.

Maybe He didn't know then. And, who am I to decide what thoughts or emotions arose in the mind of one so not like me? I'm just another poor sinner trying to make sense of it all. But this I know for certain, this I know from the depths of my being; if He didn't know then . . .

. . . He knows now.

Winter

Winter has a subtle beauty; the crispness in the air, and the purity of a freshly fallen snow.

At the same time, I miss the smells and sounds of spring. I miss the promise of nature being renewed once again, how each young blossom becomes like a friend who has come to visit for a while and then sadly must leave as summer approaches.

I'm torn between beauty and promise.

Gratitude

I enjoyed a bowl of vegetable soup the other day during lunch. I noticed the beef chunks, celery, corn, potatoes, carrots and broth.

Then, as I took each bite I started to think about where all of this comes from and all that was sacrificed so I could be nourished.

It was a very humbling experience.

I learned that gratitude should be part of every meal. When I'm grateful, I give something back to all that sacrificed for me.

Some would also call this a prayer.

Life has a way of kicking us in the butt and handing us a pillow to sit on all at the same time.

A True Master

One who has mastered the art of enlightening others does not merely provide new information. Information alone is easily forgotten and casually disregarded when some new thing comes along to excite us.

Setting aside his own reality, the Master takes on the student's views, beliefs and life story as if they are his own. Like the student, he is confined by the same limitations and constraints his student experiences. He stands with him in the darkness searching for more light.

Unlike the student, a Master is not fooled by the illusion of darkness. Where there is limitation he points his student in the direction of possibility, where there is no access he opens a window, where there is no hope he uncovers choice.

When his task is complete, he leaves behind freedom and power the student knows as his own.

Mother's Day

Unless we are looking, we will fail to notice that creation is continuously occurring all around us.

The present moment hides nothing if you know how to look and listen.

Mothers express God's plan revealed as our ever-expanding universe.

From the merging of basic elements that form suns and planets to the majesty and complexity of the human body, it is this partnership we can observe working in perpetual motion; creation expressed through an infinite variety of forms.

To celebrate Mother's Day is also to acknowledge the vast fertility of life and the Supreme Architect who spoke it into existence.

Fatherhood

To the same extent that Mothers take care of organizing and watching over the details of day-to-day life, Fathers also play no less of an important role within the family.

Like the male whitetail deer that can be seen at dusk roaming the borders of his territory protecting his herd from intruders, the human male follows his sense of duty to protect and provide for those he loves. This is his way of showing love and mostly, it's a task that's done in solitude and with little recognition from their children.

His children will never know how many sleepless nights are spent by him worrying about paying the bills, putting money aside for college, or listening for the sound of their car finally pulling into the driveway late at night. Alone he battles the relentless demands of being and doing enough so they can rest peacefully.

Their troubles are thrown upon his shoulders so often and resolved so quietly he seems invisible. His wisdom is not received from books.

Finally, when life has used the last scrap of his energy, he passes away silently and with only a final question left unanswered on his lips, "Could I have done more?"

And those who remain behind are left wondering to themselves, "Who was he?" and "Why didn't we take the time to really know him?"

If you stop to think about it, our notion of perfection controls much of what we do, spend money on and strive for in life.

Wait For It!

It's so weird . . . things happen that at the time seem wrong, untimely and inconvenient. Then an hour, a day or month passes and suddenly the perfection of that situation is revealed to us-if we are looking for it.

What I'm working on, is to withhold judgment or criticism until the jewel of that moment is revealed to me.

Over and over again, what I learn about Life is that it's perfect, just the way it is and just the way it isn't. What appears to be imperfect is my understanding of what happens.

But from a wider perspective, even our ignorance is perfect . . .

What Really Matters

Looking back over my life it seems that possessions, power and prestige have never made much of a difference. All of these things eventually fade away as if they never existed. What remains in the void left behind is the truth of what really matters in life—if we are courageous enough to look at it.

The truth is . . . all we have is each other.

Even after we've gotten everything we want, this simple fact remains; someone out here still needs us. As long as there is one among us who is cold, hungry or suffering needlessly, our job is not done. Closing our eyes, hiding out and looking the other way will not relieve us of this sacred duty.

Ultimately, we are responsible for all of it.

Notice your reaction to what happens.
What is life trying to tell you?

The Path to Peace

A young student of life, upon noticing the wars, upset and struggle created by mankind, asked the Sage, "Why does peace never seem to last?"

"Men mistakenly believe peace can be won by force, advantage or manipulation. But such a peace is only a stalemate and therefore never lasts," said the Sage.

"Real peace is the natural expression of partnership and workability. Whether found in a friendship, within a community or among nations, when the mutual goal is partnership and workability, peace is a natural result", continued the Sage.

"How can we access partnership and workability?" the student questioned.

"By giving up our need to dominate, win, or blame others", said the Sage, "we silence our minds so partnership and workability can flourish. *Partnership* is an agreement to cooperate to advance mutual interests. *Workability* is the capability of a strategy, or plan being put into effective, which allow for a mutually desired benefit."

"Until men learn to reveal their fears and selfish intent, they will never be able to give up that which stands in the way of peace. The same can be said of friendship," the Sage said with a smile, "We must become our definition."

Final Words from the Sage

The gentle Sage stood before his four students who were sad to learn that today was to be his final day among them.

"Will you give us one final word of wisdom before you leave us?" begged the youngest with deep brown eyes that stood at his side.

After a long pause, the Sage placed his hand on the young man's shoulder, and looking lovingly into his eyes and then, spoke the two words that contained all that his wisdom could offer them.

"Serve others!" said the Master, noticing the yearning in their eyes.

"When service to others becomes who you are rather than what you feel obligated to do, it does not end when they are fed, healed, taught, enlightened, or clothed—it just finds another form of expression through you."

"Being used by the majesty of Love is the purest form of partnership with God," said the Sage as he placed his satchel on his shoulder. "Be well, my brothers, it has been my honor to serve you. I leave you now, but my love will remain with you always!"

Then he left them. Alone, with only the memory of their adventures together as his companion, he traveled eastward toward his home—never to return from whence he came.

Yes, of course, the youngest repeated to himself, *the majesty of Love.*